SMILE-A-WHILE

TEACHER JOKES

By Gary Chmielewski
Drawings by Ron G. Clark

Library of Congress Cataloging in Publication Data

Chmielewski, Gary, 1946-
  Teacher.

  (Smile-a-while joke book)
  Summary: A collection of jokes and riddles about
teachers, classrooms, and other aspects of schools and
education, including "When should teachers wear
sunglasses? When they have bright students."
  1. Education—Juvenile humor.   2. Wit and humor,
Juvenile.   [1. Schools—Wit and humor.   2. Education—
Wit and humor.   3. Jokes.   4. Riddles] I. Title.
II. Series.
PN6231.S3C46   1986   818'.5402   86-17773
ISBN 0-86592-688-3

ROURKE ENTERPRISES, INC.
VERO BEACH, FLORIDA 32964

Teacher to Student: Why would you bring your duck with you to class?
Student: I want him to be a wise quacker.

English Teacher: "What is an autobiography?"
Ron: "I know! I know! It's the life story of a car!"

Math Teacher: "If I cut a steak into two parts, what would I get?"
Gail: "Halves."
Teacher: "Right, and then cut in half again?"
Gail: "Quarters."
Teacher: "And again?"
Gail: "Eighths."
Teacher: "And again?"
Gail: "Hamburgers!"

What did Pat do when his puppy chewed up her dictionary?
She took the words right out of his mouth.

Rita: "Mom, I learned to write in school today."
Mother: "What did you write?"
Rita: "I don't know, I haven't learned to read yet!"

Teacher: "Did your mother help you with your homework?"
Tanya: "No."
Teacher: "Are you sure?"
Tanya: "Yes, she didn't help me – she did it all!"

Math Teacher: "If you put your hand in your right pocket and found 75¢, and then put your hand in your left pocket and found 50¢, what would you have?"
George: "Someone else's pants!"

Mother: "Julie, why are you crying?"
Julie: "My teacher yelled at me for something I didn't do."
Mother: "What was it you didn't do?"
Julie: "My homework!"

What animal runs around the classroom stealing answers?
A Cheetah.

What is a warlock's favorite subject?
Spelling!

Why did the teacher date the new custodian?
He swept her off her feet.

How do you like school?
Closed!

Student: "Is it true that the law of gravity keeps us on this earth?"
Teacher: "Yes."
Student: "What did we do before the law was passed?"

Teacher: "What's the matter, Tommy?"
Tommy: "I don't want to scare you, but my mother said if I didn't get better grades, someone is going to get punished!"

"Mother, could you help me with my homework?"
"It wouldn't be right."
"I know – but you could at least try!"

Teacher: "Why are you running?"

Boy: "I'm running to stop a fight."

Teacher: "Between who?"

Boy: "Me and the guy who's chasing me!"

Teacher: "Laura, I hope I didn't see you looking over at Christy's test."

Laura: "I hope so too."

Were the test questions hard?
No, the questions were easy. It was the answers that were hard!

What marks did you get in physical education last year?
I didn't get any marks, only bruises!

What's a snake's favorite subject?
Hiss-tory.

Billy's Mother: "Billy told me he got 100 on his tests yesterday."
Counselor: "He did. A 50 in spelling and a 50 in arithmetic."

Teacher: "This is the fifth time this week I've had to punish you. What do you have to say for yourself?"
Chuck: "Thank goodness it's Friday!"

Father: "What does this 'F' on your report card mean?"
Son: "Fantastic!"

When should teachers wear sunglasses?
When they have bright students.

Teacher: "A, B, C, D, E, F, G. What comes after G?"
Gary: "Whiz!"

Teacher: "Tom, you've been late to school every day since school began. What's the reason?"

Tom: "I can't help it. The sign on the street says, 'School. Go Slow'."

Teacher: "Wendi, name the capital of every state."
Student: "Washington, D.C.!"

Why can't you whisper in school?
It's not aloud!

Where is your homework paper?
You won't believe this, but I made a paper airplane out of it and
someone hijacked it!

Teacher: "Well, there's one good thing I can say about your son."
Father: "Oh? What's that?"
Teacher: "With grades like his, he can't possibly be cheating!"

Counselor: "How are your marks in school?"
Student: "Under water."
Counselor: "What do you mean?"
Student: "Below C-level!"

Mother: "I know my daughter talks a lot in class, but she is trying."
Teacher: "She sure is!"

Student: "I don't think I deserve a zero on this test."
Teacher: "Neither do I, but it's the lowest grade I can give you!"

English Teacher: "John, your spelling is terrible. Don't you ever read a dictionary?"
John: "No, I'll wait for the movie!"

Chemistry Teacher: "What is the formula for vanishing?"
Pupils: "Hey bub a ree bub!"
Teacher: "That's right! Oh my!"

Where is the English Channel?
I don't know, our television set doesn't pick it up!

Why do students have such good eyesight?
They're pupils.

Teacher: "Children, open your geography books. Who can tell me where Mexico is?"
Laura: "I know – I know. It's on page 31!"

What three words do teachers like most about their jobs?
June, July, and August.

"Teacher, I can't do this problem."
"Any six-year-old should be able to do it."
"Well, no wonder I can't. I'm ten."

Daughter: "Dad, can you write your name in the dark?"
Dad: "I think so."
Daughter: "Great. Would you please turn off the lights and sign my report card?"

English Teacher: "Who was Homer?"
Bobbie: "Didn't he invent baseball?"

Science Teacher: "Who can tell me what an atom is?"
Student: "Isn't that the guy who went out with Eve?"

Why did Charlie bake his term paper?
The teacher said he wanted it well done.

"Class, you've all been very noisy, so you'll all have to stay after school."
"Give me liberty or give me death."
"Who said that?"
"Patrick Henry!"

Science Teacher: "What is a comet?"
Student: "I don't know."
Teacher: "Don't you know what they call a star with a tail?"
Student: "Oh, sure. Lassie."

Parents: "Everything is going up – the price of food, clothing, everything. I wish something would go down."
Daughter: "Take a look at my report card!"

Why do you hate school?
I don't hate school, it's the principal of the thing!

What did one math book say to another math book?
Boy, do I have problems.

Principal: "Why are you late this morning?"
Student: "Because of the alarm clock. Everyone got up except for me."
Principal: "How was that?"
Student: "There are eight of us in the family and the alarm was set for seven!"